CW00862734

Lasagna!

Easy and Quick Mouth-Watering Lasagna Recipes!

Includes Gluten-free and Vegetarian Lasagnas!

Julien Robideaux

Copyright © 2020 Julien Robideaux

All Rights Reserved. No part of this publication may be reproduced in any form or by any means, including scanning, photocopying, or otherwise without prior written permission of the copyright holder

License Notes

•   This book is licensed for your personal enjoyment only. This book may not be re-sold or given away to other people. If you would like to share this book with another person, please purchase an additional copy for each recipient. If you're reading this book and did not purchase it, or it was not purchased for your enjoyment only, then please return to your favorite retailer and purchase your own copy. Thank you for respecting the hard work of this author.

Disclaimer

Brand named and marked ingredients are for reference only. No compensation was received or solicited. Feel free to use other manufacturer's ingredients as you may desire. These recipes for your entertainment and enjoyment. No warranty about utility or satisfaction is stated or implied. The reader accepts any and all liability when using any of these recipes and/or techniques.

Table of Contents

1. Master the Skills!

I have Good News!

Fantastic, luscious, mouth-watering Lasagnas are now well within your reach!

Healthy, nutritious lasagna dishes are easier than ever to create and with these recipes, virtually foolproof. Advances in food processing and advances in cooking techniques have made these delightful, but previously frustrating dishes, to use the vernacular, "Duck Soup" simple.

Sure, there's still a little work to be done, but that goes without saying. Onions still don't chop themselves. Garlic doesn't self-mince, although both minced and crushed garlic is available in convenient to use jars. There's even a product that has little frozen cubes of minced garlic. Each cube is one clove!

Now, you can create amazing and delightful lasagna meals without hardly mussing your hairline.

Gone are the days when you have to first boil lasagna noodles, then run the risk of tearing them or having to burn your fingers trying to arrange them.

This convenient ebook of specialty recipes contains two parallel paths to success.

The first is the traditional way: create sauces from scratch, with ingredients of your own choosing and variety.

The second is to use commercially prepared sauces and embellish them with you own personal signature improvements.

Whichever way you choose to go, this book will help guide you to extraordinary success.

A Note about Wine

Some of these recipes call for "wine". I caution you to only use "drinking" wine. Never use "cooking wine". Cooking wine is 'denatured' by adding salt. This process destroys the taste and adds unnecessary salt. The ephemeral cost savings between using drinking wine and using cooking wine, in my opinion, is not warranted. Why? In most recipes, the wine is boiled down to evaporate and remove the alcohol, leaving the tasty and subtle wine flavoring elements intact. Using cooking wine with its heavy salt load destroys this experience.

A Note about Paprika

Throughout this book, you'll see admonishments about not using "smoked" Paprika. That's my own personal preference. I do not feel that the smoky taste adds anything to these recipes. I much prefer imported sweet Hungarian paprika. Paprikas fresh from the Kalosca or Szeged regions of Hungary have subtle flavor notes that, in my opinion, enhance these recipes. The Spanish 'smoked paprikas' do not.

To increase shelf life, always store your paprika in sealed containers in the freezer.

2. Lasagna! Recipes

Lasagna is an ancient form of pasta that has its roots in the 14th century in Italy. Generally ascribed to having been created in Naples, Italy, **lasagne di carnevale** was prepared primarily for festive occasions. Our recipes have been adapted from that early embodiment.

Make all of these recipes Gluten-Free by using Gluten-Free Noodles! One good source is Barilla®.

2.1. Traditional Lasagna Recipe

Ingredients:
1 lb. lean (80/20) ground beef
¾ lb. bulk pork sausage
3 – 8 oz. cans tomato sauce
2 – 6 oz. cans tomato paste
2 garlic cloves, minced
2 teaspoons sugar
1 teaspoon Italian seasoning
1 teaspoon salt
½ teaspoon pepper
3 eggs
3 tablespoons minced fresh parsley
3 cups (24 ounces) 4% small-curd cottage cheese
1 – 8 oz. carton ricotta cheese
½ cup grated Parmesan cheese
9 lasagna noodles, cooked and drained
6 slices provolone cheese
4 cups shredded part-skim mozzarella cheese, divided

Directions:
In a large skillet, cook beef and sausage over medium heat until no longer pink.
Use a wooden spatula to break up clumps.

Add the tomato sauce, tomato paste, garlic, sugar, seasoning, salt and pepper.

Bring to a boil. Reduce heat and simmer, uncovered, for 1 hour, stirring occasionally.

Preheat oven to 375°F.

In a large bowl, combine eggs and parsley.

Stir in the cottage cheese, ricotta and Parmesan cheese.

Spread 1 cup of meat sauce in an ungreased 9X13-in. glass baking dish.

Layer with three noodles, a coating of the cottage cheese mixture, a layer of meat sauce, and a dusting of mozzarella.

Repeat to make more layers.

Top with the remaining noodles, meat sauce and mozzarella.

Cover and bake for 50 minutes.

Uncover and bake 20 minutes longer or until heated through.

Let stand for 15 minutes before cutting.

Serves 6

2.2. Quick and Easy Mexican Lasagna

Ingredients:
1 can Hunt's® tamales
1 can red kidney beans, drained
1 package spicy Monterey Jack Pepper® cheese, shredded
To Serve:
Crispy Tortilla Chips
Salsa
Spanish rice

Directions:
Preheat the oven to 375°F.
Peel the husks off the tamales and discard husks.
Place one layer of the tamales on the bottom of an 8X8-inch glass baking dish.
Pour the beans beans over the tamales, then top with shredded cheese.
Double the cheese layer for a more cheesy dish.
Bake for 20 minutes.
Serve with tortilla chips and salsa, or rice.

2.3. No-Fuss Beef Lasagna

Ingredients:
1 lb. lean (85/15) ground beef or lean bulk Italian Sausage
¼ teaspoon garlic salt
1 jar Classico® Italian Sausage Pasta Sauce or your own Sugu
1 – 14.5 oz. can San Marzano diced tomatoes, undrained
3 cloves garlic, crushed, minced
1 – 15 oz. carton part-skim ricotta cheese
¼ cup Romano cheese, grated
1 egg, beaten
10 no-boil lasagna noodles
4 cups part-skim mozzarella cheese, shredded, divided

Directions:
Heat oven to 375°F.
In 12-inch skillet over medium heat, stir-cook the beef over medium heat until no longer pink.
Use a wooden spatula to break up clumps.
Season beef with salt and stir in spaghetti sauce, tomatoes and garlic. Set aside.
In 2 qt. mixing bowl, whisk together ricotta cheese, Parmesan cheese and egg.
Ladle 2 cups beef sauce over bottom of 9X13-inch baking dish.
Arrange four lasagna noodles lengthwise in single layer.
Place a fifth noodle across end of baking dish, breaking noodle to fit dish; press noodles into sauce. Spread a layer of ricotta cheese mixture over noodles.
Sprinkle with 2 cups mozzarella cheese and top with 1½ cups beef sauce.
Arrange remaining noodles in single layer; press lightly into sauce.
Top with remaining beef sauce, cheese, ricotta, and mozzarella.
Bake 45 minutes or until noodles are tender.
Sprinkle remaining mozzarella cheese on top.
Tent lightly with aluminum foil.
Let stand 15 minutes before cutting.
Serves 6

2.4. Lasagna alla Bolognese

Ingredients:
For the ragu:
½ lb. lean (85/15) ground beef
½ lb. ground Italian sausage
2 slices of pancetta, chopped
½ carrot, finely chopped
½ celery stalk, finely chopped
1 small yellow onion, finely chopped
a handful of parsley, leaves and stalks finely chopped
¼ teaspoon garlic salt
white wine to cover (about half a bottle of drinking, NOT cooking wine)
1 – 8 oz. can Contadina® tomato sauce
1 – 6 oz. can Contadina® tomato paste

Directions:
Prepare the Ragu:
In a medium soup pot over medium heat, stir-cook the beef over medium heat until no longer pink.
Use a wooden spatula to break up clumps. Remove to a serving bowl and set aside.
Turn down the heat to low and add the pancetta.
Once the pancetta begins to melt, add the carrot, celery, onion and parsley.
Season with a pinch of salt then let cook until the vegetables are soft.
Return the meat to the pan, season with another pinch of salt and add the wine to cover.
When the wine has reduced by half, add the tomato and a tablespoon or two of water.
Cover and simmer for 2-3 hours.
The result should be a thick, glossy, tasty ragu. Add a little more water if the ragu seems too dry.

For the bechamel and assembly:
3½ tablespoons butter
½ cup flour

2 cups cold milk
3½ oz. finely grated Parmesan cheese
1 lb. lasagna noodles, cooked al dente, rinsed, drained, and dried on paper towels.

Directions:

Make the bechamel sauce: melt butter in a medium saucepan.
Fold in the flour, a little at a time.
Stir with a wooden spoon to create a light tan roux.
Blend in the milk and stir until smooth.
Cook until the sauce just clings to and coats the back of the spoon.

Assemble the lasagna:
Preheat the oven to 350°F.
Use a 9X13-inch rectangular or 8X8-inch square glass casserole dish.
Ladle some ragu on the bottom and spread out to the edges.
Cover with a single layer of lasagna noodles.
Spead on a layer of ragu. Then ladle on a layer of bechamel.
Sprinkle a layer of Parmesan Cheese.
Continue layering until dish top is reached.
Sprinkle the top with a heavy coating of Parmesan cheese.
Bake for about 30-45 minutes.
The lasagna should be golden brown with sauce bubbling at the edges.
Let rest 15 minutes before cutting.

2.5. Crockpot Mexican Lasagna

Ingredients:
12-14 corn tortillas
2 cups of shredded Mexican 4-cheese blend
1 tablespoon of Fajita Seasoning (recipe below)
1 – 28 oz. can crushed tomatoes
1 – 15.5 oz. can of black beans, drained
1 – 15.5 oz. can sweet corn kernels
2 cups of mild Pace® Picante salsa
2 cups of cooked rotisserie chicken, boned, shredded
1 small yellow onion, chopped
Sour cream or Avocado for garnish

Directions:
Spray 4 qt. automatic crockpot with cooking spray.
Cover the bottom of the liner a layer of tortillas.
Next, spread a layer of tomatoes on the tortillas.
Sprinkle some chopped onions on top of the tomatoes.
Spread a layer of black beans over all.
Cover beans with a layer of salsa.
Apply a generous dusting of Fajita Seasoning.
Next layer on the chicken.
Cover chicken with a layer of corn.
Top corn with a layer of shredded cheese.
Cover all with a layer of tortillas.
Repeat the layering.
Continue layering until near the top of the slow cooker.
Finish with a layer of tortillas.
Cover with the rest of the tomatoes and cheese.
Cook on 'automatic' for 4 hours.
Serve, topped with sour cream or avocado

Fajita Seasoning
Ingredients:
1 tablespoon dark chili powder
1 tablespoon ground cumin

1 tablespoon crushed Mexican oregano
1 tablespoon garlic powder
1 teaspoon salt
½ teaspoon freshly ground black pepper

Directions:
Place all ingredients in a sealable glass jar.
Seal and shake vigorously to mix.

2.6. Mexicali Down Home Lasagna

Ingredients:
1 lb. lean (80/20) ground beef
1 large red onion, diced
Guadalajara Seasonings Mix (recipe below)
1 – 4½ oz. can sliced black olives
1 – 4 oz. can Ortega® diced green chiles
1 – 16 oz. can black beans, drained and rinsed
1 – 15 oz. can Hunt's® tomato sauce
1 – 14½ oz. can Hunt's® choice –cut tomatoes, drained
1 – 12 oz. jar Ortega® mild salsa
10 corn tortillas
16 oz. grated 4-cheese Mexican blend

Directions:
Brown meat in a 12-inch, non-reactive, deep sided skillet.
Add onion and cook until slightly caramelized.
Add Guadalajara Seasonings Mix and stir into meat and onions.
Add next five ingredients and stir to heat through.
In the bottom of a 4qt. Slow Cooker, add a single layer of tortillas.
Top with enough meat mixture to just cover tortillas.
Sprinkle with cheese.
Add another tortilla layer and repeat.
Continue to layer until all of the meat mixture is used up.
Add a final layer of tortillas and top with a layer of cheese.
Cover and cook on LOW for 3-4 hours.
Cut into wedges and serve with garnishes of your choice.
Serves 4

Guadalajara Seasonings Mix
[for 1 lb. ground beef]

Ingredients:
¼ teaspoon Spanish Paprika (not smoked)
1½ teaspoons ground cumin

1 teaspoon Mexican Oregano powder
2 teaspoons dark chili powder
1¼ teaspoons onion powder
¼ teaspoon cane sugar
½ teaspoon garlic powder
1 teaspoon crushed red pepper flakes

2.7. Slow Cooker Italian Lasagna

Ingredients:
1 lb. lean (80/20) ground beef
1 medium yellow onion, chopped
4 cloves garlic, minced
1 – 29 oz. can tomato sauce
1 – 6 oz. can tomato paste
1½ teaspoons finely ground Himalayan salt
1 teaspoon dried Mediterranean Oregano
1 – 12 oz. package lasagna noodles, uncooked
12 oz. small curd cottage cheese
½ cup grated Parmesan cheese
16 oz. shredded part slim mozzarella cheese

Directions:
In a large non-reactive deep-dish pot over medium heat, stir-cook the beef until no longer pink.
Use a wooden spatula to break up clumps.
Add onion and sauté until translucent.
Add garlic and sauté 30 seconds.
Add the tomato sauce, tomato paste, salt, and Oregano and mix thoroughly.
Stir until all are heated through.
In a large bowl mix together the cottage cheese, Parmesan cheese, and mozzarella cheese.
Using a 6 qt. automatic slow cooker, spoon a layer of the meat mixture onto the bottom.
Add a layer of the lasagna noodles. Break to fit.
Cover noodles with a layer of the cheese mixture.
Repeat the layering of sauce, noodles, and cheese.
Finish with layer of cheese.
Cover, and cook on 'automatic' setting until all are bubbly and noodles are cooked, about 4-6 hours.

2.8. South of the Border Lasagna

Ingredients:
1 lb. lean (80/20) ground beef
1 yellow onion, diced
1 tablespoon taco seasoning (recipe below)
1 – 14 oz. can black beans, rinsed & drained
1 – 14 oz. can fire-roasted diced tomatoes with green chilies
½ teaspoon salt
6-8 flour tortillas
1½ cup grated cheddar cheese
1½ cup Pepperjack® cheese
sour cream for topping

Directions:
In a large non-reactive deep-dish pot over medium heat, stir-cook the beef until no longer pink.
Use a wooden spatula to break up clumps.
Add onion and sauté until translucent.
Stir in taco seasoning, tomatoes & green chilies, black beans and salt.
Spread about ½ cup of the meat mixture into the bottom of a 4 qt. automatic slow-cooker.
Top with a tortilla.
Top with another ⅓ -½ cup meat mixture and cheese.
Repeat the layering and alternate the layers with the two different cheeses.
Cover the slow-cooker and cook on automatic setting 4 hours.
Cut into wedges and remove to serving plates.
Serve with sour cream and any other topping you like.

Taco Seasonings Mix
Ingredients:
2 tablespoons dark chili powder
1 tablespoon sweet Hungarian Paprika
1 teaspoon cumin
1 tablespoon garlic powder

1 tablespoon onion powder
1 teaspoon Mexican Oregano powder
¼ teaspoon hot Hungarian Paprika (or ¼ teaspoon crushed red pepper flakes)

Directions:

Mix all ingredients together.
Store in a sealed glass container in refrigerator.
Store in freezer for longer shelf life.

2.9. Sausage and Peppers Lasagna

Ingredients:
½ pound lean sweet ground Italian sausage
1 medium yellow onion, diced
½ cup each green and red bell peppers, cored, seeded, diced
4 cups Kraft® Shredded Low-Moisture Part-Skim Mozzarella Cheese
1 cup Kraft® Grated Parmesan Cheese
2 – 8 oz. packages Philadelphia® Cream Cheese, softened
½ cup whole milk
1 – 24 oz. jar Classico® Italian Sausage pasta sauce
½ teaspoon dried Mediterranean Oregano
12 lasagna noodles, cooked al dente, rinsed, drained, patted dry on paper towels.

Directions:
Heat oven to 350° F.
Brown sausage with onions and peppers in large skillet over medium-high heat.
Combine mozzarella and Parmesan. Reserve 2 cups.
Blend togther cream cheese and milk in medium bowl.
Add remaining cheese blend to cream cheese mixture and mix well.
Drain sausage mixture and return to skillet.
Stir in pasta sauce, meat sauce, and oregano.
Spread ⅓ of the meat sauce onto bottom of 9X13-inch glass baking dish.
Layer with 3 noodles. Place a noodle across the end of the dish, cutting it to fit.
Ladle half the cream cheese mixture over the noodles.
Add a layer of meat sauce and a layer of reserved cheese mixture.
Continue layering until all the noodles are used.
Top with the remaining meat sauce and reserved cheese mixture.
Cover with foil sprayed with cooking spray.
Bake 1 hour or until heated through, removing foil after 45 min.
Let stand 15 min. before cutting to serve.

2.10. Skillet Lasagna

Ingredients:

2 slices thick-cut bacon, diced
½ pound extra lean (85/15) ground beef
½ teaspoon finely ground Himalayan Pink salt
½ teaspoon freshly ground black pepper
2 cloves garlic, crushed, minced
1 medium yellow onion, diced
1 – 14 oz. jar pasta sauce of your choice
1 – 14 oz. can no-salt-added crushed tomatoes
½ cup water
¼ teaspoon crushed red pepper flakes
2 teaspoons dried Italian Seasonings
6 oz. dry lasagna noodles, broken into squares
½ cup ricotta
½ cup mozzarella, shredded
¼ cup basil, roughly chopped

Directions:

In a 12-inch deep-sided skillet set over medium heat, cook bacon until just crispy.
Add ground beef and season with salt and pepper.
Stir-cook the beef until no longer pink.
Use a wooden spatula to break up clumps.
Add garlic, onions, pasta sauce, crushed tomato, water, red pepper flakes, and Italian Seasonings.
Blend the mixture and then bring the sauce to a simmer.
Add lasagna noodles and cover noodles completely with the sauce.
Let cook for 15 minutes or until the noodles are soft.
Add ricotta to the lasagna and fold in gently.
cover top with mozzarella cheese.
Sprinkle with basil.
Let sit for 5 more minutes or until the cheese is melted and noodles are softened.
Serve immediately.

2.11. Spaghetti Lasagna

Ingredients:
2 tablespoons sea salt
1 lb. spaghetti
2 eggs, lightly whisked (divided)
½ cup finely grated Parmesan
1 lb. lean (80/20) ground beef
1 large yellow onion, chopped
3 garlic cloves, minced
2 tablespoons tomato paste
1 – 28 oz. can crushed tomatoes with liquid
¼ teaspoon dried Mediterranean oregano
3 cup ricotta cheese
3 cup shredded mozzarella cheese
2 tablespoon chopped Italian parsley

Directions:
Bring a large pot of salted water to a rolling boil.
Add spaghetti and cook until al dente, about 8 minutes.
Drain, rinse, and drain, then return the spaghetti to the pot.
In a small mixing bowl, whisk together 1 egg and the Parmesan and toss to combine. Set aside.
In a medium soup pot over medium-high heat, stir-cook the meat until no longer pink.
Use a wooden spatula to break up clumps.
Add onion and stir-cook until translucent.
Stir in garlic and stir-cook about 30 seconds.
Lower heat to medium and fold in tomato paste.
Stir-cook for 1 minute, then add the crushed tomatoes and oregano.
Season with salt and pepper and simmer for 10 minutes.
In a medium mixing bowl, whisk together ricotta and remaining egg.
In a 9X13-inch glass baking dish, spoon a thin layer of sauce in the bottom of the dish.

Top with half of the spaghetti noodles.
Cover with about half of the remaining sauce, half of the ricotta mixture and half of the mozzarella.
Repeat once more.
Bake until the cheese is melted and the lasagna is warmed through, about 20-30 minutes.
Garnish with parsley.
Serves 12

2.12 White Sauce Chicken Lasagna

Ingredients:
9 lasagna noodles, cooked al dente, rinsed, drained
½ cup butter
1 medium yellow onion, diced
1 clove garlic, minced
½ cup all-purpose flour
1 teaspoon garlic salt
2 cups low-sodium chicken broth
1 ½ cups whole milk
4 cups shredded mozzarella cheese, divided
1 ¼ cup grated Parmesan cheese, divided
1 teaspoon dried basil
1 teaspoon dried Mediterranean oregano
½ teaspoon freshly ground white pepper
1 pint ricotta cheese
2 cups cooked boneless, skinless rotisserie chicken meat, sliced into ¼-inch chunks
2 – 10 oz. packages frozen chopped spinach, thawed and drained between paper towels
1 tablespoon chopped fresh parsley

Directions:
Preheat oven to 350°F.
Make the White Sauce:
Melt the butter in a large saucepan over medium heat.
Stir-cook the onion until translucent.
Add the garlic and stir-cook 30 seconds.
While whisking, slowly add the flour and salt. Whisk until a light tan roux forms.
Whisk in the broth and milk until smooth.
Bring to a boil, then reduce the heat to simmer.
Blend in 2 cups mozzarella cheese and ¼ cup Parmesan cheese.
Whisk in the basil, oregano, and pepper.

Remove from heat, and set aside.

Assemble the Lasagna:

Spread ⅓ of the sauce mixture evenly over the bottom of a 9X13-inch glass baking dish.

Layer with 3 of the noodles, a thin layer of ricotta, and then top with the chicken.

Arrange 3 of the noodles over the chicken, and ladle in ⅓ of the sauce mixture,

Arrange the spinach on the sauce.

Sprinkle with the remaining mozzarella cheese and ½ cup Parmesan cheese.

Arrange remaining noodles over cheese, and spread remaining sauce evenly over noodles.

Sprinkle with parsley and the remaining Parmesan cheese.

Bake 35 to 40 minutes.

Let rest for 5 minutes, then serve.

2.13. Extra-Easy Lasagna

Ingredients:
1 lb. lean (80/20) ground beef
1 large yellow onion, diced
5 cloves garlic, crushed, minced
2 tablespoons McCormick's® Classic Italian Seasonings
1 – 14.5 oz. can Hunt's® Diced Tomatoes
2 – 23.5 oz. jars Prego® Italian Sausage and Garlic Pasta Sauce
1 – 15 oz. container whole milk ricotta cheese
½ cup large curd cottage cheese
4 cups shredded mozzarella cheese, divided
2 eggs
12 uncooked lasagna noodles
⅓ cup hot water

Directions:
Preheat oven to 350ºF.
In a non-reactive pot over medium heat, stir-cook the beef until no longer pink.
Use a wooden spatula to break up clumps.
Add onion and stir-cook until onion is translucent.
Add garlic and stir-cook for 30 seconds.
Add Italian Seasonings and diced tomatoes. Stir-cook until heated through.
Fold in both jars of pasta sauce.
Bring mixture to a rolling boil, reduce heat, and simmer 20 minutes.
In a bowl, mix together Ricotta, Cottage Cheese, 2 cups of shredded Mozzarella, 2 eggs.
Place four noodles in the bottom of a 9X13-inch ungreased glass baking dish: three side by side and one across the end to cover.
Place 1 scoop of cheese mixture on each of the four noodles.
Use a spatula to evenly spread the cheese to cover noodles.
Cover all with layer of meat sauce.
Repeat with four more noodles, cheese mix and meat.
Make four layers, finishing with the meat sauce.
Slowly pour the hot water around the inside edge of the dish.

Tightly cover baking dish with heavy-duty aluminum foil.
Bake for 1 hour.
Uncover and spread top with 2 cups shredded mozzarella.
Bake 10 more minutes until mozzarella is melted and bubbly.
Let stand 10 minutes before serving.
Serves 6

2.14. 4-Ingredient Slow Cooker Lasagna

Ingredients:
8 oz. lasagna noodles, cooked al dente, rinsed, drained, patted dry on paper towels
2 – 24 oz. jars Classico® Italian Sausage Pasta Sauce with Onions and Garlic
2 – 15 oz. containers ricotta cheese
¼ cup grated Parmesan cheese
cooking spray

Directions:
Spray a 4 qt. automatic slow cooker with cooking spray.
Ladle 1 cup of sauce over bottom of slow cooker.
Add a single layer of three noodles on top of sauce.
Break noodles to fit.
Top with about ¾ cup ricotta cheese.
Top with ½ cup sauce.
Repeat with noodles, ricotta and sauce 3 more times.
Top with 3 final noodles and one more cup of sauce.
Sprinkle with Parmesan cheese.
Cover and cook on "Automatic: for 4 hours.
Serves 4

2.15. Beefy Crockpot Lasagna

Ingredients:

1 lb. extra lean (85/15) ground beef
1 large yellow onion, chopped
4 garlic cloves, crushed, minced
1 – 28 oz. can Hunt's® tomato sauce
1 – 6 oz. can tomato paste
1½ teaspoon garlic salt
1 teaspoon dried Mediterranean oregano
12 oz. small curd cottage cheese
½ cup grated Parmesan cheese
12 oz. lasagna pasta, uncooked
16 oz. shredded mozzarella cheese

Directions:

In a non-reactive pot over medium heat, stir-cook the beef until no longer pink.
Use a wooden spatula to break up clumps.
Add onion and stir-cook until onion is translucent.
Add garlic and stir-cook for 30 seconds.
Add tomato sauce, tomato paste, salt and oregano.
Bring to a simmer and heat through.
Spoon a layer of meat sauce onto the bottom of a 6 qt. Automatic Slow Cooker.
Add a crossed double layer of uncooked lasagna noodles (break to fit) and top with cheeses.
Repeat with sauce, noodles and cheeses until all are used up.
Cover and cook on "Automatic" for 4 to 5 hours.
Serves 4

2.16. American-Style Lasagna

Ingredients:
½ lb. extra lean (85/15) ground beef
4 cloves garlic, minced
1 – 14½ oz. prepared spaghetti sauce of your choice
1 tablespoon turmeric powder
½ teaspoon freshly ground black pepper
1 tablespoon sweet Hungarian paprika
1 teaspoon McCormick's© Perfect Pinch® Italian seasonings
¼ cup water
6 uncooked lasagna noodles
1 cup small curd cottage cheese
1 egg
½ cup Parmesan cheese, divided
2 cups Mozzarella cheese, shredded, divided

Directions:
Preheat oven to 350°F.
In a non-reactive pot over medium heat, stir-cook the beef until no longer pink.
Use a wooden spatula to break up clumps.
Add onion and stir-cook until onion is translucent.
Add garlic and stir-cook for 30 seconds.
Blend in spaghetti sauce, turmeric, pepper, paprika, Italian seasonings, water.
Continue to cook, stirring until sauce becomes fragrant.
Spoon ⅓ meat sauce over bottom of ungreased 8X8-inch glass baking dish.
Top with 3 noodles. Break noodles to fit.
Mix the cottage cheese, egg and ¼ cup Parmesan cheese.
Spoon half of cheese mixture over noodles.
Top with ⅓ of meat sauce. Top meat sauce with ½ of Mozzarella cheese.
Layer remaining noodles.
Spoon remaining cheese mixture over noodles.
Cover with remaining meat sauce.

Top with remaining Parmesan and Mozzarella cheeses.
Be sure noodles are covered with sauce and topping.
Bake for 50 to 60 minutes until lasagna is bubbly, lightly browned and noodles are done.
Serves 4

2.17. No-Boil Classic Lasagna

Ingredients:
1 lb. lean (80/20) ground beef
2 – 23.5 oz. jars Prego® Italian Sausage and Garlic Pasta Sauce
2 eggs
9 uncooked no boil lasagna noodles
2 cups large curd cottage cheese (or 1 – 15 oz. Ricotta cheese)
3 cups shredded mozzarella cheese, divided
½ cup Parmesan cheese

Directions:
Preheat oven to 350°F.
In a non-reactive pot over medium heat, stir-cook the beef until no longer pink.
Use a wooden spatula to break up clumps.
Stir in both jars of pasta sauce.
Bring to a boil, reduce heat, stir, and simmer 20 minutes.
In a bowl, mix together Cottage Cheese, Parmesan cheese, 2 cups Mozzarella cheese, 2 eggs.
In a 9X13-inch glass baking dish, spread 1 cup of meat sauce.
Place 3 lasagna noodles over sauce.
Spread ⅓ of the cheese mixture over noodles.
Top with ⅓ of the meat sauce.
Repeat to form 3 layers.
Top with remaining meat sauce.
Tightly seal with foil.
Bake 1 hour.
Uncover, sprinkle with reserved Mozzarella cheese.
Bake an additional 5 minutes or until cheese is bubbly.
Remove from oven and let rest 15 minutes before serving.
Serves 6

2.18 Hearty Vegetable Lasagna

Ingredients:

1 – 16 oz. package lasagna noodles, cooked al dente, rinsed, drained, dried between paper towels
1 lb. fresh mushrooms, sliced
¾ cup green bell pepper, cored, seeded, ribbed, diced
1 small yellow onion, diced
3 cloves garlic, minced
2 tablespoons extra-light olive oil
2 – 26 oz. jars marinara sauce of your choice
1 teaspoon dried basil
1 – 15 oz. container part-skim ricotta cheese
4 cups shredded mozzarella cheese, divided
2 large eggs
½ cup grated Parmesan cheese

Directions:

Preheat oven to 350°F.

Prepare the Mushroom sauce:

Bring a large saucepan to temperature over medium heat, add oil and bring to shimmering.

Add mushrooms and stir-cook until most of the moisture has evaporated.

Add the onions and stir-cook until translucent.

Add the bell peppers and stir-cook until softened.

Add the garlic and stir-cook for 30 seconds.

Blend in pasta sauce and basil and bring to a boil. Reduce heat, and simmer 15 minutes.

Assemble the Lasagna:

In a 2 qt. mixing bowl, blend together ricotta, 2 cups mozzarella cheese, and eggs.

Spread 1 cup of mushroom sauce across the bottom of a greased 9X13-inch glass baking dish.

Add a layer of cooked noodles, and spread a thin layer of ricotta mix over all.

Cover with a thin layer of mushroom sauce and Parmesan cheese.

Repeat layering until all the noodles have been used, and top with remaining mozzarella cheese.

Bake, uncovered, for 40 minutes until lasagna is bubbly and top is golden.

Let stand, covered, for 10 minutes before serving.

Serves 6

2.19. Lasagna Rollups Di Napoli

Ingredients:
1 – 15 oz. Ricotta cheese
1 cup shredded mozzarella cheese
¼ cup Parmesan cheese
1 – 10 oz. package frozen spinach, thawed, and well-drained.
1 egg
1 – 23.5 oz. jar Prego® Italian Sausage and Garlic Pasta Sauce
9 Lasagna noodles, cooked al dente, rinsed and drained

Directions:
Preheat oven to 350ºF.
In a 3 qt. mixing bowl, mix together all cheeses, spinach, egg.
In an 8X8-inch glass baking dish, pour ½ cup of pasta sauce.
Using a suitably covered work surface, spread ⅓ cup cheese mixture on each lasagna noodle.
Roll up noodles and place on pasta sauce in baking dish, seam side down.
Pour remaining pasta sauce over all.
Cover with aluminum foil.
Bake for 35 minutes.
Remove from oven and let rest 10 minutes before serving.
Serves 4

2.20. Lasagna for One

Ingredients:
1 – ¼ pound patty precooked Black Angus beef, diced, crumbled
1 – 11 oz. jar Prego® Italian Sausage and Garlic Pasta Sauce
½ cup Hunt's® Diced Tomatoes
1 teaspoon McCormick's® Perfect Pinch© Italian Seasonings
1 teaspoon Avocado oil
1 small yellow onion, diced
5 cloves garlic, crushed, minced
1 egg
2 uncooked lasagna noodles, broken in half
½ cup large curd cottage cheese (or Ricotta cheese)
2 cups shredded mozzarella cheese, divided
⅓ cup hot water

Directions:
Preheat oven to 350ºF.
In a non-reactive pan, heat Avocado oil and stir-cook onion until translucent.
Add garlic and cook for 30 seconds.
Add Italian Seasonings and Diced Tomatoes. Stir-cook to heat through.
Stir in pasta sauce and meat.
Bring to a boil, reduce heat and simmer 10 minutes.
In a bowl, mix together Cottage Cheese, 1 cup of shredded Mozzarella, egg.
Pour ¼ cup pasta sauce over bottom of a miniature disposable foil pan.
Place 1 noodle piece in the bottom of the pan.
Spread ¼ of the cheese mixture over the noodle.
Top with ¼ of the sauce.
Repeat to make at least 4 layers, finishing with meat sauce.
Slowly pour water around inside edge of pan.
Tightly cover baking dish with heavy-duty aluminum foil.
Bake for 1 hour.
Uncover and spread top with 1 cup shredded mozzarella.

Bake 10 more minutes until mozzarella is melted and bubbly. Let stand 10 minutes before serving.

2.21. Lasagna-Stuffed Shells

Ingredients:
1 lb. lean (80/20) ground beef
½ medium onion, finely chopped
2 garlic cloves, crushed
½ teaspoon salt and ⅛ teaspoon freshly ground black pepper, as you may desire
¼ cup red wine (any kind), optional
1 – 25 oz. jar of marinara sauce, divided
5 oz. package of fresh spinach, chopped
16 oz. reduced fat ricotta cheese
2 cups shredded mozzarella cheese, divided
2 large eggs
2 tablespoons chopped fresh parsley
⅔ of a 12 oz. box jumbo pasta shells
(you will need 24 shells plus a couple extra in case any break while boiling).

Directions:
Preheat oven to 375°F.
Cook pasta shells al dente according to package instructions then drain and re-fill the pot with cold water; set aside. The cold water will stop the cooking process and prevents the shells from sticking to each other. A teaspoon of olive oil to the drained shells will accomplish the same thing.
In a non-reactive pot over medium heat, stir-cook the beef until no longer pink.
Use a wooden spatula to break up clumps.
Add onion and stir-cook until onion is translucent.
Add garlic and stir-cook for 30 seconds.
Season with salt and pepper as you may desire.
Stir in ¼ cup red wine (if using) and simmer until wine is almost completely evaporated.
Stir in ½ cup marinara sauce and chopped spinach.
Cook until spinach is wilted then remove pan from heat to cool slightly.

In a large mixing bowl, stir together ricotta cheese with 1 cup shredded mozzarella cheese.

Add eggs and chopped parsley. Stir in the meat mixture.

Pour ½ cup marinara into a 9X13-inch glass baking dish and spread over the bottom.

Drain shells and fill each one with an ice cream scoop of filling (2 rounded tablespoons).

Closely nestle pasta shells into the prepared baking dish.

Pour remaining marinara evenly over the tops of the stuffed shells.

Sprinkle the top with remaining mozzarella cheese.

Cover with foil and bake 45 minutes.

Remove foil and bake additional 3-5 minutes or until cheese is golden.

Serves 4

2.22. Lasagna di Carnevale

Ingredients:
1 batch of Ragu alla Napoletana (see recipe in **Sauces and Specialty Items**)
1 batch Meatballs di Carnevale (see recipe in **Sauces and Specialty Items**)
3 eggs, hardboiled, sliced
2 – 15 oz. containers ricotta cheese
4 cups mozzarella cheese, shredded
2 cups Parmesan cheese, shredded
12 oz. lasagna noodles, cooked al dente, well-drained on paper towels
cooking spray

Directions:
Preheat the oven to 350°F.
Coat the bottom of a 9X13-inch glass baking dish with Ragu.
Place 3 noodles side by side across the bottom of the baking dish.
Place a 4th noodle across the bottom of the 3 noodles. Press into the Ragu.
Spoon a layer of ricotta across the noodles.
Layer on another ladle of Ragu.
Distribute meatballs and egg slices across the Ragu.
Sprinkle mozzarella and Parmesan cheese over all.
Repeat layering with the rest of the noodles, meatballs, eggs, cheeses and sauce.
Finish with a Ragu/cheese layer.
Cover with aluminum foil coated with cooking spray on the lasagna side.
Bake the lasagna for about 45 minutes.
Remove foil and bake another 15 minutes, until the top begins to brown.
Let cool, uncovered, at least 30 minutes, then serve.
Add more mozzarella as you may desire.

2.23. Seafood Lasagna

Ingredients:
12 lasagna noodles, cooked, drained on paper towels
3 tablespoons Avocado oil, divided
1 medium yellow onion, diced
1 – 8 oz. package Philadelphia® brand cream cheese, softened
1 – 15 oz. container Ricotta cheese
1 egg, beaten
1 tablespoon fresh basil, ribs removed
½ teaspoon finely ground Himalayan Pink salt
⅛ teaspoon freshly ground white pepper
2 – 10.75 oz. cans Campbell's® condensed cream of mushroom soup
⅓ cup whole milk
⅓ cup dry sherry
1 – 6 oz. can lump crabmeat, drained
1 lb. cooked salad shrimp, deveined, tails removed
¼ cup grated Parmesan cheese
½ cup shredded sharp Cheddar cheese
2 cups mozzarella cheese, shredded
2 cups fresh sliced button mushrooms

Directions:
Heat 2 tablespoons Avocado oil in a medium sauté pan over medium heat.
Add onion and cook and stir until translucent.
Blend in cream cheese, Ricotta, egg, basil, and salt and pepper.
In a medium mixing bowl, combine soup, milk, and sherry.
Fold in crab, shrimp, and mushrooms.
Place 3 noodles side by side in the bottom of a well-oiled 9X13-inch glass baking dish.
Cross the bottom of the dish with a 4th noodle.
Spread ¼ cheese mixture over the noodles.
Spoon ¼ soup mixture over cheese.
Spread ½ cup mozzarella cheese over soup mixture.
Repeat in layers until noodles are used up.
Finish with soup mixture.

Bake, uncovered, at 350°F. for 45 minutes.
Top with Cheddar and Parmesan cheeses.
Brown lasagna under broiler.
Remove from oven, and let stand 30 minutes before serving.

2.24 A Fantastic White Sauce Lasagna

Ingredients:
Meat Sauce:
1 tablespoon extra light olive oil
1 medium yellow onion, finely chopped
1 carrot, peeled, finely diced
4 cloves garlic cloves, minced
1½ lb. lean (85/15) ground beef
½ lb. lean ground pork
1 – 24 oz. can diced tomatoes, pureed, strained
1 – 14 oz. can crushed no salt added tomatoes
3 tablespoons tomato paste
2 teaspoons granulated beef bouillon
1 tablespoon dried Italian Seasonings
½ teaspoon sugar
Garlic salt and freshly ground black pepper as you may desire
White Sauce (Béchamel):
¼ cup butter, softened
¼ cup all-purpose flour
3½ cups whole milk, divided
1 cup fresh shredded parmesan
Lasagna:
1 – 16 oz box no-boil lasagna noodles
3 cups mozzarella cheese, shredded
2 tablespoons finely chopped fresh parsley

Directions:
Meat Sauce:
Bring a medium soup pot to temperature over medium heat then add beef and pork.
Stir-cook until no longer pink, using a wooden spatula to break up clumps.
Fold in the onion and carrots and stir-cook until onion is translucent and carrots are softened.

Add garlic and stir-cook 30 seconds.

Fold in the next 6 ingredients (pureed tomatoes through sugar).

Bring to a rolling boil, then reduce the heat and simmer 25 minutes.

Dust with salt and pepper as you may desire.

When slightly thickened, remove from heat and set aside.

White Sauce (Béchamel):

In another medium soup pot, melt butter over medium heat.

Gradually whisk in the flour to form a light tan roux.

Reduce heat down to low and gradually whisk in the milk, pouring it in a thin stream.

Continue whisking until a smooth, creamy sauce forms without lumps.

If the sauce is too thick, add a little more milk as you may desire.

Increase heat to medium.

Continue stir-cooking the sauce until thick enough to coat the back of a wooden spoon.

Dust in the parmesan cheese and remove from heat.

Season with salt and pepper and mix until the cheese is melted through.

Putting it all Together:

Preheat oven to 350°F.

Spread 3/4 cup of meat sauce over the inside bottom of a 9x13-inch baking dish.

Arrange a layer of lasagna noodles on top of the sauce.

Spread a thin layer of meat sauce over the noodles.

Spread 1 cup of white sauce over the meat sauce, and dust with half of the mozzarella cheese.

Repeat layers until the noodles are all used up.

Spread the remaining meat sauce and white sauce over the last layer of noodles.

Top with the remaining mozzarella cheese.

Bake for 25 minutes or until golden and bubbling.

Garnish with parsley.

Let rest, uncovered, for about 10 minutes before slicing and serving.

3. Sauces and Specialty Items

Here is a collection of stand-alone recipes for foodstuffs that either can be used in other embodiments, or are stand-alone items used in recipes found in this book. I've collected these together in one place, although they may be referenced in more than one recipe: saves duplicating sub-recipes.

Some of these delicacies, like the Ragú and the Meatballs, are complete recipes in their own right. By separately cataloging them, you have the ability and freedom to use them in your own, signature perfections.

3.1. Classical Italian Sausage Pasta Sauce

Ingredients:
¼ cup ground mild Italian Sausage
1 red bell pepper, cored, seeded, diced
1 green bell pepper, cored, seeded, diced
1 – 6 oz. can tomato paste
1 – 15 oz. can tomato sauce
1 – 14.5 oz. can diced tomatoes
1 tablespoon white cane sugar
1 medium yellow onion, diced
5 cloves garlic, crushed, minced

Directions:
In a non-reactive pot, brown the sausage. Do not drain.
Add onions and stir until translucent.
Add peppers and stir until softened.
blend in the rest of the ingredients.

Bring to a boil. Lower heat and simmer 1 hour, covered.
Makes approximately 5 cups sauce

3.2. Amy's Sugu

Ingredients:
¼ pound lean (85/15) ground beef
1 medium yellow onion, chopped
Salt and freshly ground black pepper as you may desire
1 – 6 oz. can tomato paste
3 tomato paste cans of water
½ teaspoon sugar
2 bay leaves
½ teaspoon fennel seed

Directions:
In a non-reactive pot over medium heat, stir-cook the beef until no longer pink.
Use a wooden spatula to break up clumps.
Add onion and stir-cook until onion is translucent.
Add salt and pepper as you may desire.
Add tomato paste, water, and remaining ingredients.
Cover and cook over medium heat 1 to 2 hours. Stir occasionally.
Discard bay leaves and serve.

3.3. Sicilian Spaghetti Sauce

Ingredients:
2 – 15 oz. cans tomato sauce
1 – 6 oz. can tomato paste
1 – 4 oz. can sliced mushrooms with liquid
1 tablespoon McCormick's® Perfect Pinch Italian Seasonings
1 teaspoon chopped bird's eye peppers
1 teaspoon hot Hungarian paprika
1 cup low-sodium chicken broth

Directions:
Combine all ingredients in a large saucepan.
Cook for 2 hours, stirring occasionally.
Makes 6 cups

3.4. Fajita Seasoning

Ingredients:
1 tablespoon dark chili powder
1 tablespoon ground cumin
1 tablespoon crushed Mexican oregano
1 tablespoon garlic powder
1 teaspoon salt
½ teaspoon freshly ground black pepper

Directions:
Mix all ingredients together.
Store in a sealed glass container in the refrigerator.
Store in the freezer for longer shelf life.

3.5. Guadalajara Seasonings Mix

This makes enough Mix to season 1 lb. of ground beef.

Ingredients:
¼ teaspoons Spanish paprika (not smoked)
1½ teaspoons ground cumin
1 teaspoon Mexican Oregano
2 teaspoons dark chili powder
1¼ teaspoons onion powder
¼ teaspoon cane sugar
½ teaspoon garlic powder
1 teaspoon crushed red pepper flakes

Directions:
Mix all ingredients together.
Store in a sealed glass container in the refrigerator.
Store in the freezer for longer shelf life.

3.6. Taco Seasonings Mix

Ingredients:
2 tablespoons dark chili powder
1 tablespoon sweet Hungarian Paprika
1 teaspoon cumin
1 tablespoon garlic powder
1 tablespoon onion powder
1 teaspoon Mexican Oregano powder
¼ teaspoon hot Hungarian Paprika (or ¼ teaspoon crushed red pepper flakes)

Directions:
Mix all ingredients together.
Store in a sealed glass container in the refrigerator.
Store in the freezer for longer shelf life.

3.7. Ragù alla Napoletana

- **Ingredients:**
- 1 lb. ground sirloin
- 1 lb. ground pork rib meat
- 8 oz. ground mild Italian pork sausage
- 1 small yellow onion, finely chopped
- 2 tablespoons tomato paste
- ⅓ cup Lambrusco® wine
- 3 – 14 oz. cans San Marzano® crushed tomatoes
- handful fresh basil leaves
- salt and freshly ground black pepper as you may desire

Directions:
- Heat a medium, non-reactive pot and brown the meats.
- Add the onion and cook until translucent.
- Stir in the tomato paste and wine and bring to a boil.
- Continue to cook until the volume of the liquid is reduced by one-third.
- Add the tomatoes and basil, season with salt and freshly ground black pepper and stir well.
- Bring to a boil, then lower the heat to a simmer.
- Cover and cook, stirring occasionally, for about an hour.
- Add additional wine if the mixture seems too dry.

3.8. Meatballs di Carnevale

Ingredients:
8 oz. extra lean (85/15) ground beef
8 oz. ground mild Italian sausage
¼ cup Panko-style Italian flavored breadcrumbs
¼ cup Parmesan cheese
1 egg
¼ cup water
Garlic salt and freshly ground black pepper as you may desire
flour, for dredging
Extra-light olive oil for frying

Directions:
In a suitable mixing bowl, combine the first 6 ingredients (beef through water).
Add salt and pepper as you may desire.
Knead thoroughly, then form into small individual meatballs, about ¾-inch to 1-inch in diameter.
Place a small amount of flour in a shallow bowl.
Roll meatballs around to lightly coat with flour.
Heat about ½ cup of oil in a 12-inch, deep sided, non-reactive frying pan.
Fry the meatballs in batches until golden brown, rolling them around in the oil to fry all sides.
Drain on paper towels.

4. How to Keep Your Knives Sharp

How to Sharpen a Knife Like a Professional - Part 1 - Selecting a Stone

More people get knife cuts from dull knives than from sharp knives. The reason is very simple: dull knives tend to slide off what they are intended to cut, and then cut what they're not supposed to - like fingers, and hands. Keeping your knives as sharp as possible is the way to keep from getting cut. But like most things, doing it right takes skill and some direction. Knife sharpening is not something that you can do haphazardly. This monograph will take the mystery out of how to get professional results when you sharpen your knives.

First some terminology: Knives come in three basic "flavors": Stainless Steel, High Carbon, and Ceramic. Knives come in two basic edge configurations: Serrated and Straight. Sharpening equipment comes in two configurations: automatic and manual. Most professionals prefer manual sharpening equipment. Manual sharpening equipment comes on many shapes and types. There are three types that we'll focus on in this paper: Arkansas Stones, Ceramic hones, and Steels. The most common of these is the Sharpening Steel. A long pointed rod, it has ribs running the full extent of the Steel.

All knife sharpening methods are the same: a small amount of the knife blade material is removed while the blade is shaped to form a cutting edge. All sharpening equipment perform the same basic action - remove that small amount of material while creating that cutting edge.

Before we begin, I must caution you - never attempt to sharpen a Ceramic knife blade. The material, typically a fused form of Zirconium Silica, is incredibly sharp, incredibly strong, and incredibly brittle. Only diamond sharpening tools are used to form the cutting edge on a Ceramic blade. I caution you to not try to sharpen a Ceramic blade at home. Buy a new one and discard the dull one. Never fear, it takes a lot of cutting to dull a Ceramic blade!

Before we get to actually sharpening the knife, let's check the blade by using a bright light source, preferably like a pin spot in the ceiling. Hold the knife in front of you, parallel to the ground, with the sharp edge up and see if you can see any 'shiny' spots on the cutting edge when you hold the blade under the light. A truly sharp blade won't have any 'shiny spots'. If you see these spots along the blade, the blade is a candidate for sharpening.

Now, hold the flat side of the blade parallel to the ground. Look at the cutting edge. All straight knives have their blades ground in one of two conditions: hollow ground, which is a concave that is cut into the blade for its entire length, and the straight bevel blade, where the blade is flatly shaped into a cutting surface. If you look very close along the side of the sharp edge, you will see a very narrow flat that runs the length of the blade, right along the edge. This is the actual cutting bevel, and its that bevel that you will be sharpening.

The act of sharpening the blade is the removal of equal parts of metal from that very narrow flat along the edge. You grind down that narrow bevel until the 'shiny spots' you saw above go away. The actual grinding operation, the 'sharpening' operation requires very little force, but it does require some precision. I prefer manual sharpening to machine sharpening. You have more control over the sharpening process when you do manual sharpening. The selection of the type of stone to use is more of an individual preference and technique than of actual 'goodness' or 'badness'.

Choosing a Stone: Most Knife purists swear by the Arkansas Stone. The Arkansas Stone comes in two basic types: a rough surface for fast cutting and a fine surface for securing the edge. All **Arkansas Stones** are used "wet", that is, either a liquid like oil or water is used on the stone while the blade is being sharpened. The reason is simple: as the stone wears away the unwanted metal from the blade, some stone material is removed from the face of the stone. These miniscule particles of stone and metal fill up and clog the pores the stone, reducing its ability to sharpen. The liquid removes these worn-away particles and keeps the stone surface in cutting order. I prefer to always wet whatever I'm using to sharpen. That way I know I have a fresh cutting surface to work with.

For myself, I prefer the **round Ceramic Rod**. I treat it like an Arkansas Stone, using water as a lubricant. And I roll it like one rolls a Steel. I find I can get a smoother edge, but that's just my preference.

Diamond infused stones have always been somewhat of a gimmick to me: for one thing, the size of the sintered diamonds is usually inconsistent in lower cost sharpening surfaces, and their ability to smoothly grind an edge seems to be harder to master.

Sharpening Steels: These have been the traditional blade sharpening tool for all around use. Cheap to produce, they are usually a little harder than the blade, so they sharpen the blade faster than they wear down. Being denser than stones, they don't usually pick up and hold water, but they do hold oil fairly well.

The next section, we'll explore how to use these manual stones.

How to Sharpen a Knife Like a Professional - Part 2 - Manual Sharpening

Sharpening a blade using a Steel: (for right-handed people) - Place the handle of the Steel in your left hand and hold the Steel vertical, point down. Place the point on a cloth or other suitable surface. Hold the knife in your right hand and starting at the heel [the part of the sharp edge closest to the handle], place the blade at the top of the Steel, and draw the knife blade down the Steel while drawing the knife blade back away along the Steel. Properly done, the point of the knife will leave the Steel at just about the bottom of the Steel. Keep the angle of the knife blade to the Steel the same angle as the thin bevel, so the thin bevel draws smoothly across the edge of the ribs of the Steel. You want to grind away metal from only the thin small bevel edge, not the whole width of the blade.

Make one draw on the right side of the Steel, then one draw on the left side of the Steel. Rotate the Steel about ¼ turn as you draw the blade across the edges of the Steel's ribs. You'll see people in restaurants using the Steel and blade by holding the Steel up in the air. I don't recommend this except for show: for one thing, it's impossible to hold the correct angle on the bevel, and for another, the pressure of the Steel against the blade is totally uncontrollable. You'll dull the knife far faster than sharpen it with this showy, but impractical, technique.

A tip for the experienced: As you gain experience, you may want to try this variation on a theme: Now the object to getting a sharp edge is the uniform removal of material from each side of the blade. Typically, this means alternating on each stroke from one side of the Steel to the other. However, here's a tip - as long as the amount of strokes is the same on one side as on the other, you can 'double up' strokes. For a typical Stainless Steel knife, I'll make, say 30 strokes on the left side, turn the blade over and then make 30 strokes on the right side. Then I'll make 25 strokes on the left side, turn it over and then do 25 on the right. I'll reduce the number of strokes by 5 on each side until I get down to the last 5 strokes. Then I'll do 2 strokes on one side, 2 strokes on the other side, 1 stroke on one side and 1 one stroke on the other, and repeat that last set, 3 times. Then I'll rinse and dry the blade, and look at it's edge under a bright light. I should not see any 'shiny spots'. And the knife will be razor sharp.

Sharpening a blade using a Ceramic Rod: (for right-handed people) - follow the same techniques as with a Steel. Be sure to keep the Rod wet. But be careful - the Rod, like all Ceramic pieces, is brittle, and can snap if addressed too aggressively. The Ceramic Rod will give you a finer finish on the blade, and a smoother cutting edge than a Steel.

Sharpening a blade using a Stone: (for right-handed people)- this becomes a little trickier. Typically flat stone sharpening is done with the stone laid, well, flat. The stone is still kept wet, but now there's nothing to hold onto on the stone to keep it where it is. Again, the challenge is to stroke the blade along the stone from heel to point, holding the bevel angle constant. Experts disagree whether the blade should be stroked towards you, so the material flows off the sharp edge, or stroked away from you, so the material flows back across the body of the blade. Personally, I like to stroke the blade away from me.

In either case, the 'flat stone' technique necessitates changing hands with the blade so that alternate strokes sharpen alternate sides of the blade. This, in my book, makes for an uneven finish and an uneven sharpening bevel. I use a flat stone only as a last resort.

How to Sharpen a Knife Like a Professional Part 3 - Miscellaneous Notes and Observations

In an emergency, like - you get called upon to carve the Thanksgiving Turkey at your in-laws. You find that the knives they offer you need some really fine touchup to give them a good edge, and nowhere is there a knife sharpener, even an old worn Steel. There's an old Chef's tip that you can use: The unglazed rim on the bottom of a china saucer makes a good temporary sharpening surface. Be sure to keep it wet, and perhaps don't let the hostess see what you're doing. Be careful, tho. An unglazed piece of terra cotta pottery won't sharpen a blade. Nor will a surface like a natural stone such as travertine. An unpolished section of granite countertop should be used only in an extreme emergency!

Stainless Steel blades, although bright and shiny, don't hold an edge very well. The metal in the blade is surprisingly soft when compared to even the mildest of Round Steaks. Plan to resharpen stainless steel blades every time you use them. If you feel some pulling while you're cutting with a stainless steel blade, resharpen at once. Don't get me wrong: I use a stainless steel vegetable knife for fine and delicate cuts, but I have to 'stone' it every time I use it.

High carbon steel is the best knife edge, but knives made from this material have to be washed and dried after every use - they will rust fairly quickly when left in a pan of water during dinner. Leaving them in a dishwasher can lead to rust spots. A rusted blade has to be polished before use, otherwise the rusted and stained areas will drag while cutting and ruin a smooth cut.

Very high carbon steels, such as are found on old straight shaving razors, last the longest, have the sharpest cutting edge, and are fine instruments. In truth, the straight razor does not rely on the sharpness of the steel to do its extraordinary cutting job: the act of 'sharpening' a straight razor is merely wearing down of the steel to expose the carbon filaments within the metal matrix. These carbon filaments are incredibly sharp. The filaments point every which way, so the act of "stropping" the blade (drawing the blade back and forth across a piece of smooth leather), breaks off the carbon filaments so that what's left all point the same direction.

Looking at the edge of a well-stropped straight razor through a magnifying glass, you'll see an edge that looks like a miniature saw blade. It's this sawing action that causes the razor to "glide" through the tough hairs of a beard. Did you know that the hair in a man's beard is about as tough as a copper wire of the same diameter? High carbon steel knife blades also exhibit this exposed row of carbon filaments, only to a lesser extent. That's why it's easier to cut through something with a slight sawing motion instead of trying to push the knife through the object. Unfortunately, Stainless Steel knife blades don't have that same characteristic.

If you find a knife that is stamped "Old File" or a name like that, buy it. It will probably be hand forged. This is a blade made from exactly what it says - an old file. It will be a high carbon steel, it will hold an edge exceedingly well, and will last you a lifetime.

A last word: always try to buy a blade that's forged, not stamped. Forged blades are stronger, denser, tougher, hold an edge longer, and are the hallmark of a quality blade. Stamped blades don't measure up.

5. Slicing and Dicing Onions

Onions come in many types. There's White, Yellow, Mayan Sweets, Vidalia Sweets, Red, and a range of local variations. All are diced the same way. We'll use yellow onions to illustrate.

To prepare onions, this procedure is the easiest to follow:

1. Cut the onion in half

2. Trim off the dry stalk end, leaving the root end intact.

3. Remove the dry outer layers and one "wet" layer.

4. With a sharp knife, make vertical slits from the root end to the stalk end every ¼ -inch.

5. For traditionally prepared onions, cut off the root end. The onion will separate into thin slivers just right for cooking.

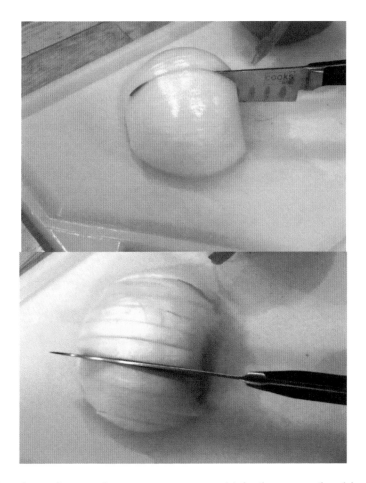

To dice the onion, make cross cuts every ¼-inch across the thin longitudinal slices. Then remove the root.

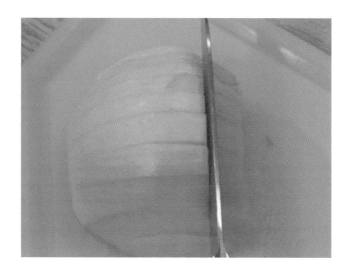

6. The Final Word

Hey everybody, just wanted to say **THANK YOU** again for checking out my latest book, *Lasagna!*

This book is exactly what you've been looking for.

I know the very first thing after you've read this book all the way through, you'll want to rush into your kitchen and start creating your special pastas. If you run into any issues or you've got questions, or you've got new ideas on how to improve these recipes with your own special touches, I'd love to hear about them.

Simply drop me a line at jrobideaux8@gmail.com.

I need to ask you a favor.

You can make a big difference.

Without a big publisher's budget for ads and PR, I depend on reviews to sell books. That little number showing how many reviews and stars each book has received is by far the best sales tool we have.

I cherish and depend upon my committed readers.

Honest reviews help other readers determine whether they should try my books, and I would be very grateful if you could take five minutes to leave me your thoughts on the product page.

Thank you so much for spending time with me and my recipes in *Lasagna!*

In gratitude,

---

7. Bonus Recipes

I know you're busy!

And I know that you took the time to capture this book.

So, in return for your kindness, I've included a few extra recipes that expand the theme of this book, and that you might just find amusing. You might discover a recipe that you can adapt to your own style.

It would give me great pleasure if you totally embraced one of these, made it your own signature dish, and then tweaked it to make it you very own unique dish!

7.1. Garlic Lamb Chops

Ingredients:
5 lbs. rack of lamb
8 cloves garlic, peeled and minced
2 tablespoons virgin olive oil
1 teaspoon freshly ground black pepper
1 teaspoon Kosher salt

Directions:
French the ends of the lamb rack:
Cut away suet, fat, etc., from the bone ends just past the center chop area.
Scrape the bones clean and cover the bare bone with foil.
Preheat your gas grill to 550°F.
Mix together the garlic, oil, pepper, and salt.
Thoroughly rub the lamb with the garlic oil mixture.
Grill the lamb on all sides to your desired degree of doneness, about 10-15 minutes.
Use an instant reading thermometer to determine when the rack reaches 145°F.

Cool the rack 5 minutes, then cut into chops before serving.
Serves 6

7.2. Grilled Salmon with Citrus Salsa Verde

Ingredients:

2 large Navel oranges
¼ cup extra-virgin olive oil
¼ cup fresh lemon juice
½ cup fresh flat-leaf Italian parsley, chopped
2 green onions, thinly sliced
3 tablespoons fresh mint leaves, chopped
2 tablespoons Mediterranean capers, rinsed, drained and coarsely chopped
2 tablespoons orange zest
1 teaspoons lemon zest
1 teaspoon crushed red pepper flakes
Avocado oil for oiling the salmon
4 – 4 oz. center cut salmon fillets, skinned
4 tablespoons amber agave nectar
Finely ground Himalayan Pink salt as you may desire
Freshly ground white pepper as you may desire

Directions:

For the salsa verde: With a sharp knife, slice off about ¼-inch from each end of the oranges.
Place an orange upright on one end.
Make a vertical cut downward along each segment, separating it from the others.
Peel the membranes and end rime off of each segment.
Place the freed segments in a non-reactive mixing bowl and slice into quarters.
Repeat with the second orange.
Add the next nine ingredients (olive oil through red pepper flakes) in the bowl.
Toss lightly and season with salt and pepper as you may desire. Set aside.
For the salmon: Preheat a gas grill to medium-high.

Brush the salmon on both sides with Avocado oil to keep the salmon from sticking.

Brush the salmon on both sides with the agave nectar.

Dust with salt and pepper as you may desire.

Grill until the fish flakes easily and is cooked through, about 3 to 4 minutes on each side.

Transfer the salmon to a serving platter and let rest for 5 minutes.

Slice and remove to individual serving plates.

Ladle the **salsa verde** over the salmon.

Provide more **salsa verde** as an accompaniment.

Serves 4

7.3. Grilled Garlic-Lime Chicken

Ingredients:
Juice of 1 lemon
1 tablespoon lime juice
¼ cup Avocado oil, divided
1 clove garlic, crushed, minced
¼ teaspoon cumin powder
2 boneless, skinless chicken breasts
Finely ground Himalayan Pink Salt as you may desire
Freshly ground white pepper as you may desire

Directions:
Preheat your gas grill to medium-high heat.
Wash chicken with lemon juice. Rinse and pat dry with paper towels.
In a bowl, whisk together lime juice, 2 tablespoons oil, garlic and cumin.
Brush chicken with the remaining oil.
Dust with salt and pepper as you may desire.
Place chicken on hot grill.
Baste with garlic-lime mixture on each side during cooking.
Grill until chicken is no longer pink inside and juices run clear.
Serves 2

7.4. Bourbon Honey Baby Back Ribs

Ingredients:
1 cup Bourbon whiskey
½ cup clover honey
3 tablespoons apple cider vinegar
2 teaspoons freshly ground black pepper
2 teaspoons onion powder
2 slabs pork baby back ribs, 3 pounds each
1 tablespoon kosher salt
¼ cup plus 1 tablespoon Avocado oil, divided

Directions:
Heat your gas grill to medium-low(300°F-325°F).
Place the Bourbon in a saucepan on the grill's heated sidecar burner.
Bring to a boil and cook, stirring occasionally, until reduced to about ½ cup, 6 to 8 minutes.
Stir in the honey, vinegar, pepper and onion powder.
Cook, stirring occasionally, until slightly syrupy, about 5 minutes.
Remove the pan from the heat.
Rub the ribs with the salt and brush with oil.
Wrap each slab separately in heavy-duty aluminum foil, wrapping tightly to form a packet.
Place on grilling grate, and cook until the ribs are tender and done, about 1½ hours.
Turn the packets occasionally.
Carefully remove packets from the grilling grate and open them on a cutting board.
Brush the grilling grate with the remaining 1 tablespoon oil.
Increase the heat to medium-high (375°F to 400°F).
Remove the ribs from the foil, and arrange on the grilling grate.
Cook, basting often with the Bourbon sauce, until a crust forms on the outside of the ribs.
Remove the ribs, and brush with the Bourbon sauce.

Cut the ribs between the bones, and serve with the remaining Bourbon sauce.
Serves 6

7.5. Traditional Potato Salad

Ingredients:
3 lb. small white potatoes
2 tablespoons salt
8 oz. jar Best Foods® mayonnaise
8 oz. Del Monte® sweet pickle relish
3 tablespoons juice from a Bread and Butter pickle jar
1 stalk celery, finely sliced
1 medium yellow onion, chopped

Directions:
Place the potatoes and salt in a large pot of water.
Bring the water to a boil, then lower the heat and simmer for 10 to 15 minutes.
Potatoes will be barely tender when pierced with a knife.
Drain the potatoes in a colander.
Place the colander with the potatoes in the empty pot.
Cover with a clean, dry kitchen towel.
Allow the potatoes to rest for 15 to 20 minutes.
Cut potatoes in quarters or in half, depending on their size.
Place the cut potatoes in a large bowl.
Add mayonnaise, relish, pickle juice, celery, onion.
Gently toss to make a smoothly blended salad.
Refrigerate for a few hours to allow the flavors to blend.
Serve cold.

7.6. Balsamic-Honey Glazed Salmon

Ingredients:

½ cup sweet balsamic vinegar (at least 9 gms sugar per serving)
2 tablespoons chicken broth
2 tablespoons Dijon mustard
2 tablespoons clover honey
5 garlic cloves, crushed, minced
1 tablespoon virgin olive oil (not "extra virgin")
8 salmon fillets (6 oz. each)
½ teaspoon finely ground Himalayan salt
½ teaspoon freshly ground black pepper
1 lemon, quartered

Directions:

Preheat oven to 400°F.
Combine the first six ingredients (vinegar through oil) in a non-reactive, deep sided saucepan.
Stir briskly and bring to a boil.
Cook until glaze is reduced and thick.
Place salmon skin-side down on a greased 15X10-inch rimmed baking pan.
Sprinkle with salt and pepper as you may desire.
Spoon glaze over salmon.
Bake, uncovered, until fish flakes easily with a fork.
Serve with wedge of lemon.
Serves 8

7.7. Grilled Szechuan Steak

Ingredients:
1 – 8 oz. London Broil steak
2 tablespoons extra light olive oil, for grilling
Marinade:
1 teaspoon minced fresh ginger
2 cloves garlic, minced
½ teaspoon crushed dried Tianjin (Tien Tsin) chiles
1 green onion, thinly sliced
1 tablespoon sesame oil
Shallot Sauce:
1 tablespoon peanut oil
1 shallot, minced
½ teaspoon minced fresh ginger
½ teaspoon minced garlic
½ teaspoon crushed dried Tianjin (Tien Tsin) chiles
1½ tablespoons low-sodium beef stock
1½ tablespoons low-sodium soy sauce
1½ tablespoons Mirin
1 tablespoon butter, melted
½ teaspoon fine table salt
½ teaspoon ground red Szechuan peppercorns, crushed, seeds and stems discarded

Directions:
Combine the Marinade ingredients in a small mixing bowl.
Place a sheet of plastic film on a suitable work surface.
Center the steak on the film and rub the steak all over with the marinade.
Wrap up the steak in the film and refrigerate 6 hours or overnight.
Make the Sauce:
In a medium saucepan, heat the oil to shimmering over low heat.
Add the next 6 ingredients (shallot through mirin) and stir-cook until the shallot is translucent.
Fold in the butter and stir-cook until the butter is fully incorporated.
Remove to a gravy bowl and keep warm.

Prepare the Steak:
Heat a gas grill to 550°F.
Remove the steak from the refrigerator, unwrap, and let it come to room temperature.
Wipe off any excess Marinade with paper towels and discard.
Brush the steak all over with oil.
Combine the salt and crushed Szechuan peppercorns and liberally rub all over the steak.
Use your fingers to press the mixture into the meat.
Grill steak to medium rare (internal temperature 120°F.), turning once.
Remove to a serving platter, let rest 15 minutes, then slice thinly across the grain.
Pour the Sauce over all and serve.

7.8. Texas-Style Beef Short Ribs

Ingredients:
2.5-3 pounds meaty beef short ribs
1 large yellow onion, sliced
water
1 teaspoon Lawry's™ Garlic Salt
1 teaspoon freshly ground black pepper
Heinz™ Classic Thick and Sweet BBQ Sauce

Directions:
Preheat oven to 350°F.
In a large, non-reactive soup pot, place the ribs and onion and add enough water to cover.
Add Garlic salt and pepper.
Bring to a rolling boil and boil for 30 minutes. Discard bones as they release from the meat.
Remove ribs from pot and place them in a 8X8-inch foil-lined glass baking pan.
Discard onion slices and cooking water.
Liberally lather ribs with BBQ sauce.
Bake, uncovered, for 60 minutes, basting with the hot BBQ sauce as the spirit moves you.
Turn off the oven.
Let the ribs rest in the oven for 30 minutes before slicing.

Cook's Note: For added flavor, reserve the onions, drained and dried on paper towels, then cover the bottom of the 8X8 pan before adding the ribs. Continue to cook as per recipe.

7.9. Chicken Santorini

Ingredients:

1 cup ricotta cheese

⅛ teaspoon dried Mediterranean oregano 'flowers'

2 teaspoons chopped green onions

⅛ teaspoon Kosher salt

¼ teaspoon freshly ground white pepper

4 boneless, skinless chicken breast halves

½ teaspoon garlic powder

2 tablespoons extra-extra light olive oil [I prefer grape oil – less taste impact]

1 cup crushed Roma tomatoes

1 cup fresh marinara sauce (I prefer Bertolini™ brand)

4 slices mozzarella cheese

Directions:

Preheat the oven to 350°F.

In a blender or food processor, combine the ricotta with the oregano, green onions, salt, and pepper. Process to blend.

Rub the chicken with the garlic powder. Heat the oil in a large skillet over medium-high heat.

Add the chicken and cook for 12 minutes per side.

Place the chicken breasts, side by side, in a large baking dish and allow to cool.

Spoon ¼ cup of the cheese mixture, ¼ cup marinara sauce, and ¼ cup crushed Roma tomatoes onto each chicken breast.

Top each chicken breast with 1 slice mozzarella.

Bake for 20 minutes, or until a thermometer inserted in the thickest portion of a breast register 170°F and the juices run clear.

Serves 4

7.10. Bistecca alla Fiorentina

Ingredients:
1½ lb. T-bone or Porterhouse steak, cut from the rib with the bone.
2 tablespoons virgin olive oil
Sea salt and freshly ground black pepper as you may desire
Lemon wedges for garnish
1½ cups baby arugula

Directions:
Take the meat out of the refrigerator about 2 hours before cooking.
Let rest, covered, on the kitchen sideboard. That guarantees room temperature meat.
Prepare a charcoal or gas grill for direct grilling over medium-high heat.
Oil the grill rack.
Rub the meat on both sides with the olive oil. (Do not add any salt at this point.)
Using tongs, lay the steak directly over the hottest part of the fire, about 5 inches above the fire.
Cook until browned and juicy on the first side, 5 to 7 minutes.
Using tongs, turn the steak and sprinkle with salt.
Cook on the second side until browned and juicy, 5 to 7 minutes more.
Then turn the meat over once again and sprinkle with salt.
Transfer the steak to a cutting board and season generously with pepper.
Let rest 5 minutes, covered.
Garnish with lemon wedges and the arugula and serve immediately.
Serves 2.

8. About Julien Robideaux

Julien Robideaux' family still calls Bourgogne, France, home. This ancient and famous area of east-central France, commonly known as "Burgundy", has produced some of the finest wines and the most creative French chefs.

Julien studied at a small gastronome not far from the Collège de Sorbonne, where he perfected his unique style of creamless sauces and roulades.

After emigrating to Quebec, Canada, Julien worked for a time as a Sous-chef for a boutique specialty cooking school within walking distance to the prestigious Academie Culinaire.

Julien now calls Southern California, home, and has embraced the famous American Southwest cuisine. Although Julien continues to travel widely in Europe, his heart, he says, has been captivated by America.

Lasagna! was inspired by the overwhelming acceptance of his previous Mediterranean-themed ebook, "***Smart Italian Cooking for Busy People!***". This volume incorporates suggestions from you, our readers, and includes an updated outline format to make it easier to find specific recipes.

These recipes all adhere to Julien's penchant of providing easy-to-prepare recipes specifically tailored for your hectic lifestyles.

9. Other Books by Julien Robideaux

Published:

Easy & Fast Gluten-Free Mediterranean Cuisine

The Little Book of Culinary Delights

Chile Diabolique: Create like a Chilihead without…

The Unofficial Recipe Book of PIGS: Exotic Recipes…

Chinese if You Please: Delicious, Simple, Fresh Wok…

Quick and Easy 1 Pot Dishes

The PIGS Paleo Diet Book: Exquisitely Delightful Recipes …

Classic Hungarian Goulashes

Fast and Easy French Cooking for Busy People-YES! You CAN do it!!!

The New Little Book of Culinary Delights

The Ketogenic Diet Plan: Can Diabetes be reversed? Drop up to 15 pounds in 10 days!

Smart Italian Cooking for Busy People-YES! You CAN do it!!!

Paleo!- Eat and Grow Smart!

New York Street Food for Busy People: Yes! You CAN do it!

Revolutionary Recipes: Early American Fare, Colonial Recipes adapted for Modern Times

Quick & Easy International Recipes: YES! You CAN Create Mediterranean!

It's All About Chicken! Poultry in Motion!

It's All About Chicken! Poultry in Motion! (Paperback)

French Cooking Made Easy! Your Taste Buds Will Love You!!

The Best Ever Holiday Dinner Recipes!

The Best Ever Holiday Dinner Recipes! -(Paperback)

Fast and Easy French Cooking for Busy People-YES! You CAN do it!!!-(Paperback)

Turmeric - The Ancient Miracle Spice

Turmeric - The Ancient Miracle Spice (Paperback)

Cooking for One: You CAN Do it!

Another Cooking For One!

Mastering Lasagnas and Spaghetti
25 Strings of Excellent Culinary Delights!
It's All about Tomatoes!
The Best Ever Thanksgiving Dinner
Recipes that Rock!!!!
Fast and Easy Greek Cooking for Busy People-YES! You CAN do it!
Fast and Easy Greek Cooking for Busy People-YES! You CAN do it! (Paperback)
The Best Ever Christmas Dinner Recipes!
Fast and Easy Japanese Cooking for Busy People-30 Unique recipes! YES! You CAN do it!
Fast and Easy Tuscan Cooking for Busy People
Fast and Easy Tuscan Cooking for Busy People (Paperback)
I Can't Believe it's THAT Easy!
I Can't Believe it's THAT Easy! (Paperback)
Forever Stroganoff!
Ditch the Salt - Not the Savor!
Ditch the Salt - Not the Savor! (paperback)
The Complete Cooking for One Cookbook!
The Complete Cooking for One Cookbook! (paperback)
How to Cook the Perfect Hard-Boiled Egg!
How to Cook the Perfect Hard-Boiled Egg! (paperback)
The Chef's Companion
The Chef's Companion (paperback)
Pasta Secrets!
Pasta Secrets! (paperback)
Cooking with Paprika!
Cooking with Paprika! (paperback)

Upcoming In the Near Future:
Tips for Successful Wok Cooking

10. Connect with Julien Robideaux

I really appreciate your reading my book! Here are my social media coordinates:

Friend me on Facebook: https://www.facebook.com/julien.robideaux

Follow me on Amazon at: http://www.amazon.com/-/e/B014LGT3xI

Connect with me at: jrobideaux8@gmail.com

Printed in Great Britain
by Amazon

71703512R00046